# GREEN FARMING

**Daniel Johnson and Samantha Johnson**

**Children's Press®**
An imprint of Scholastic Inc.

**Content Consultant**
Jeslin Varghese, LEED AP, WELL AP
President & Director of Sustainability
GBRI

Library of Congress Cataloging-in-Publication Data
Names: Johnson, Daniel, 1984– author. | Johnson, Samantha, author.
Title: Green farming / by Daniel Johnson and Samantha Johnson.
Description: First edition. | New York : Children's Press, an imprint of Scholastic Inc., 2024. | Series: A true book: a green future | Includes bibliographical references and index. | Audience: Ages 8–10. | Audience: Grades 3–5. | Summary: "This STEM-based set of True Books introduces students to the engineering innovations that can help us reach more environmentally friendly goals"— Provided by publisher.
Identifiers: LCCN 2023018943 (print) | LCCN 2023018944 (ebook) | ISBN 9781339020877 (library binding) | ISBN 9781339020884 (paperback) | ISBN 9781339020891 (ebk)
Subjects: LCSH: Sustainable agriculture—Juvenile literature. | Agriculture—Environmental aspects—Juvenile literature. | Food industry and trade—Environmental aspects—Juvenile literature. | BISAC: JUVENILE NONFICTION / Science & Nature / Environmental Conservation & Protection | JUVENILE NONFICTION / Science & Nature / General (see also headings under Animals or Technology)
Classification: LCC S494.5.S86 J65 2024  (print) | LCC S494.5.S86  (ebook) | DDC 338.1—dc23/eng/20230426
LC record available at https://lccn.loc.gov/2023018943
LC ebook record available at https://lccn.loc.gov/2023018944

Copyright © 2024 by Scholastic Inc.
All rights reserved. Published by Children's Press, an imprint of Scholastic Inc., *Publishers since 1920.* SCHOLASTIC, CHILDREN'S PRESS, A TRUE BOOK™, and associated logos are trademarks and/or registered trademarks of Scholastic Inc.

The publisher does not have any control over and does not assume any responsibility for author or third-party websites or their content.

No part of this publication may be reproduced, stored in a retrieval system, or transmitted in any form or by any means, electronic, mechanical, photocopying, recording, or otherwise, without written permission of the publisher. For information regarding permission, write to Scholastic Inc., Attention: Permissions Department, 557 Broadway, New York, NY 10012.

10 9 8 7 6 5 4 3 2 1            24 25 26 27 28

Printed in China  62
First edition, 2024

Design by Kathleen Petelinsek
Series produced by Spooky Cheetah Press

**Front cover: This farm uses solar panels to generate electricity.**

# Find the Truth!

**Everything** you are about to read is true *except* for one of the sentences on this page.

Which one is **TRUE**?

**T or F**  Organic food costs less than non-organic food.

**T or F**  Green farms avoid giving animals antibiotics.

Find the answers in this book.

# What's in This Book?

**Introduction** .................................................. **6**

## 1 Greener Crops
What are the most sustainable
ways to grow crops? ....................................... **11**

## 2 Happier, Healthier Animals
How can livestock make farms greener? .......... **21**

This Earth Day button is from 1970.

## Farming Is a Business
Is it harder to make a profit
using sustainable methods? ........................... **28**

This electric tractor drives itself!

## 3 Eco-Friendly Equipment
Will new technologies change the way we farm?............ 31

**Spot On!** ................ 40
**Take Action** ............. 42
**True Statistics** .......... 44
**Resources** .............. 45
**Glossary** ............... 46
**Index** .................. 47
**About the Authors** ...... 48

Drones can be used to check crops.

## INTRODUCTION

Farming, also known as **agriculture**, began about **12,000 years ago**. For much of that time, families grew just enough food to feed themselves. As populations grew, more people moved to towns and cities. They no longer grew their own food. So **farmers planted more crops** and began **selling them** to others.

The earliest known farms were in the Middle East and parts of Egypt in an area called the Fertile Crescent.

Combines are used to harvest wheat on a large-scale farm.

Today there are nearly 8 billion people in the world! The average farm now covers **hundreds of acres of land**. The farming methods these **large-scale industrial farms** use produce a lot of food. But they also **use a lot of resources** and make **a lot of pollution**. That is taking a toll on the environment and human health.

There are ways to produce food that **do not harm the planet**. Some farmers are using **sustainable**, or "**green**," farming methods. These practices grow crops and raise livestock in ways that are better for the environment—and offer consumers **healthier options**. Green farms might **reduce water use** by **capturing rainwater** in tanks. Or they might **use animal waste** to **generate electricity**. Read on to learn more about how farming is going green!

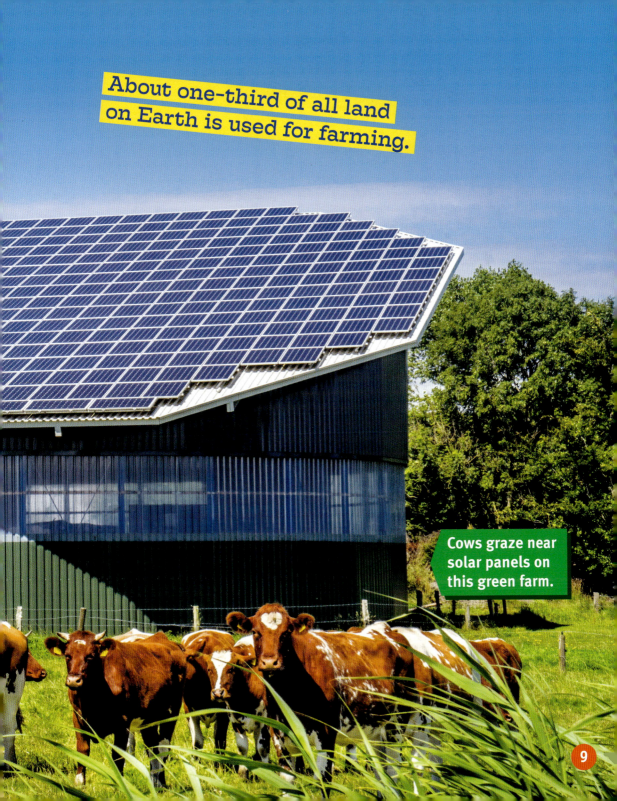

About one-third of all land on Earth is used for farming.

Cows graze near solar panels on this green farm.

People around the world get most of their daily nutrients from just three crops: wheat, rice, and corn.

Globally, more corn is grown than any other crop.

**CHAPTER**

# Greener Crops

There are about 30,000 types of plants on Earth that people can eat. But we farm only a few hundred of them. We grow even fewer as our main sources of food. That is because it is easier for industrial farms to focus on growing a single crop. No matter where they are grown, plants need space, sunlight, nutrients, and water, plus protection from pests and weeds. To provide these things without harming the environment, green farms find ways to work with nature to help crops thrive.

## Plant Food

Fertilizer is a substance that contains nutrients and is added to the soil to help plants grow. Industrial farms use **synthetic** fertilizers, which can pollute nearby water and harm wildlife. On the other hand, green farms make sure crops have the nutrients they need by using natural fertilizers such as **compost** or animal manure—otherwise known as poop—usually from cows and chickens. They may also raise worms to munch on food and animal waste. The worms leave behind nutrient-rich poop that is used as fertilizer.

Chemical fertilizer

Natural fertilizer

Chemical pesticide

Ladybugs can eat about 50 to 60 insects per day.

Natural pesticide

## Pest Control

There are many insects, like beetles, caterpillars, and aphids, that like to eat plants. Industrial farmers spray chemical pesticides to kill these unwanted visitors. But pesticides contaminate the soil and nearby water sources. They can also cause health problems in animals and humans. Green farmers may release insects, like ladybugs, into fields instead. These predators feast on unwanted bugs. Farmers may also cover crops with netting to keep harmful bugs out.

Corn crops (left) and bean crops (right) complement each other.

Farmers have been rotating crops since ancient times.

## Switching It Up

Industrial farms often plant the same crop in the same field year after year. Eventually, the soil will no longer contain the nutrients the crops need. Green farms avoid this problem by rotating, or changing, crops each year. For example, corn takes a lot of nitrogen from soil. Beans return nitrogen to soil. Rotating crops that complement each other keeps nutrients from getting used up quickly. That means farmers do not have to use as much fertilizer to replace lost nutrients.

## Keep Out!

Weeds take resources like water, nutrients, and space away from crops. Industrial farms typically use chemical herbicides to kill weeds. Instead, green farmers might cover the ground between rows of crops with wood mulch or straw. That acts like a barrier to stop weeds from growing. Green farmers may also plant cover crops in fields that are not in use. The crops will not be harvested, but they will keep fields from getting overrun by weeds. Cover crops also prevent erosion, which happens when bare soil is swept away by wind or water.

Alfalfa (right) is commonly used as a cover crop.

## More Variety

You might find one or two types of tomato, lettuce, or apple at the grocery store. Even though there are many kinds of each fruit and vegetable, industrial farms grow only a few. That can be a problem because the same plants can get the same diseases. An illness sweeping through a crop can lead to a food shortage. Green farms grow many varieties of plants—from striped tomatoes to purple carrots. That preserves a larger variety of a food—and these crops could also be more resistant to certain diseases.

These heirloom tomatoes were grown on a green farm. "Heirloom" indicates it is a traditional variety not used in industrial farming.

Today organic foods can be found in just about every grocery store.

## Certified Organic

Some fruits and vegetables at grocery stores around the world are labeled "organic." This indicates that the food has been grown on a green farm. Farmers need to follow many rules and guidelines to get this certification. Usually, the food has to be grown using no synthetic fertilizers or pesticides. In addition, organic farmers cannot use **GMO** seeds. These seeds, used in industrial farming, are typically modified to make plants resistant to certain diseases, or to work with specific herbicides.

Hydroponic farms use up to 10 times less water than traditional farms.

Hydroponic farmers can grow food year-round—even in winter.

## Saving Resources

Some green farmers are able to grow lots of food in less space by using hydroponics to farm indoors. Hydroponics is when plants are grown in water instead of in soil. The farm is inside a large building, where plants grow in racks that stack to the ceiling. Special light bulbs shine on the plants to mimic the sun. The plants' roots dangle into water filled with nutrients. The water can be reused again and again. Indoor farmers do not have to worry about pests or weeds. They can even grow crops in the middle of a city.

# Rooftop Gardens

Indoor farming is not the only way to grow food in the middle of bustling cities. People are also starting to plant green farms on the roofs of buildings! Here are some of the benefits of rooftop gardens.

- Planting on rooftops uses space that would otherwise be wasted.

- The food grown does not have to be shipped from distant farms, so less energy is used for transportation.

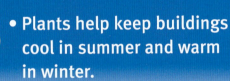
- Plants help keep buildings cool in summer and warm in winter.

- Plants soak up rainwater to reduce runoff. Otherwise, the water that ran off the rooftop would wash pollution from streets, like oil from cars, into waterways.

- Rooftop gardens provide habitats for a variety of insects and birds.

People all over the world are planting rooftop gardens.

There are about three times as many chickens in the world as people!

Livestock on green farms live a more natural lifestyle than livestock on industrial farms.

CHAPTER

# Happier, Healthier Animals

Cattle, poultry, and pigs are raised for their meat. Some cows are raised for their milk. Sheep provide wool, and chickens lay eggs. To meet the demand for these products, livestock is often raised in cramped conditions with little access to the outdoors. The many animals on a large farm or ranch need lots to eat. And they produce lots of waste. Green farms are working to raise animals in a more **humane** way—and one that takes less of a toll on the environment.

> Fish can be farmed too. There are currently no organic certifications for farmed fish in the United States.

# Natural Living

Green farms can also raise organic livestock. To obtain that certification, animals must be raised on land free of chemical pesticides and fertilizers. The livestock can only eat organic feed or graze on naturally growing plants. Hormones and other synthetic chemicals cannot be used to help them grow. And the animals must have access to clean water and bedding, sunlight and fresh air, and space to exercise.

Grass is a more natural diet for cattle than industrial feed.

Animals are not allowed to roam free on many industrial farms.

## Room to Roam

On many industrial farms, animals are kept indoors in cages, pens, and stalls. That allows farmers to check on the animals, provide food and water, milk cows, and collect chickens' eggs more easily. This is handled differently on green farms. There, animals spend part or all of their time outdoors. They have a shelter to return to in bad weather. Being allowed to roam free also means animals can interact with one another, making life less stressful.

## Waste Removal

Livestock produce billions of tons of manure a year. Rain can wash this waste into nearby waterways, polluting them. To avoid animal waste ending up where it is not wanted, green farms reuse it. Manure makes great fertilizer that can be spread on crops to help them grow. Other green farms turn livestock waste into fuel. The waste is collected in large tanks. As it breaks down, it releases methane gas that can be burned to create electricity or heat homes.

### Timeline: Milestones in the Evolution of Farming

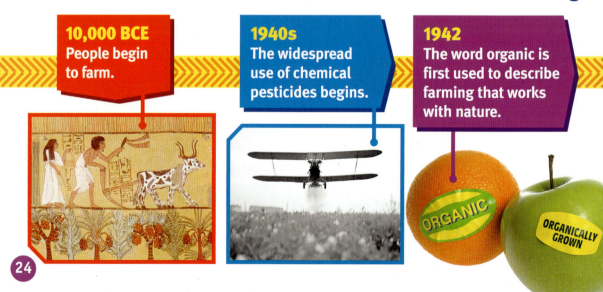

**10,000 BCE** People begin to farm.

**1940s** The widespread use of chemical pesticides begins.

**1942** The word organic is first used to describe farming that works with nature.

## Honeybees Are Livestock Too!

When you hear the word *livestock*, you probably think of big animals—cows, horses, sheep, or pigs. But some of the most important animals on a farm are tiny—like bees! Thousands of honeybees work all summer long collecting nectar from flowers to create honey. Honeybees that are raised on an organic farm make organic honey.

Honeybee

**1960s–1970s**
Environmental concerns over pesticide use arise. People become more aware of the need to protect the environment.

**1983**
Austria becomes the first country to create regulations for organic farming.

**TODAY**
There are about 3 million organic farms worldwide.

Vaccines protect animals from certain illnesses.

The first antibiotic, called penicillin, was discovered in 1928.

## Disease Prevention

Disease can spread quickly when many animals are kept together on an industrial farm. Some of these farms regularly give their animals antibiotics. These medicines kill disease-causing bacteria. But the overuse of antibiotics can lead to the development of bacteria that cannot be killed by any medicine. Instead of using antibiotics, green farms make sure the areas where animals live are kept clean to prevent the spread of disease. And they make sure animals get **vaccinated**.

# Cutting Back on Cows

Green farming fixes some problems that come with raising livestock, but not all of them. For example, cows burp a lot. Each time they do, they release methane. The cows' manure gives off methane too. This greenhouse gas traps heat from the sun in Earth's atmosphere. That adds to **climate change**. And raising livestock for food is not the most sustainable way to feed people. The grain grown to feed the animals could be used to feed people. And the land needed to raise livestock could also be used to grow crops for people. Groups like the World Health Organization suggest that raising less livestock would be healthier for people and for the planet.

Livestock accounts for more than 14 percent of all human-caused greenhouse gas emissions.

## The BIG Truth

# Farming Is a Business

There are many benefits to green farming. So why don't all farms use these practices? Here are some reasons:

### 1 Smaller Yield:
Green farms do not produce as much food as industrial farms. Fewer crops to sell means less money earned.

### 2 Higher Costs:
Sustainable farms rely on natural fertilizers and pest control, as well as organic food for livestock. These resources often cost more than synthetic fertilizers and pesticides and traditional animal feed.

### 3 More Time:
It can take at least three years before a farm can be certified organic. And farmers must put in a lot of extra effort to make sure they keep that status.

# 4

## More Work:

Sustainable farms often grow a variety of crops in small amounts. This requires more labor. It is also more work to rotate and plant cover crops to keep soil healthy. Industrial farms, on the other hand, often grow just one high-value crop. They use machinery and chemicals to make work easier.

## The Bottom Line

Green farming comes with extra effort, costs, and time. That is why organic and sustainably grown food often comes with a higher price tag. That means not everyone can afford sustainably grown food.

On average, wind turbines are as tall as a 28-story building.

Wide-open spaces make a farm a great place for wind turbines.

CHAPTER 3

# Eco-Friendly Equipment

Modern farming requires a lot of machinery. Large tractors plow fields so they can be planted. Combines harvest grain crops, like wheat. Trucks haul trailers, animals, and tools. All these machines usually run on **fossil fuels** that pollute the air and worsen climate change. That is why some green farms have switched to **renewable** sources of energy, like solar or wind power. Other green innovations allow farmers to use less water, create less pollution, and farm smarter.

## Harvesting Sunshine

Some green farms have installed solar panels that turn sunlight into electricity to light and heat barns. Farms are great places for solar **arrays**. They have lots of wide-open spaces and get plenty of sun. Some farms have enough panels to power their farm as well as hundreds of nearby homes and businesses. And installing solar arrays doesn't take land away from farming. Crops can be planted under the panels or the field can be used for grazing animals.

The use of land for agriculture and solar power is known as agrivoltaics [ag-ri-vohl-TAY-iks].

Sheep graze near a solar array.

## Wind Power

Wind power is another source of green energy for farms. Tall wind turbines have long blades that catch the wind and spin to make electricity. Wind can also be used to generate mechanical power. For example, some farms use windmills to drive pumps that draw water up from underground wells. The pumps are used to **irrigate** fields and supply drinking water for animals in pastures.

This windmill provides drinking water for livestock.

The first electric vehicle was invented in the 1800s.

A cord connects to a smart grid to provide renewable energy for this electric tractor.

## Charged Up

There are millions of electric cars on roads around the world. These vehicles are powered by batteries instead of fossil fuels. They require less energy to run and they produce less pollution than gas-powered vehicles. Farm equipment companies are now producing electric tractors for farms as well. The technology is new. But the hope is that electric tractors could replace traditional gas-powered vehicles.

# Animal Helpers

Before machines were invented, farmers relied on animals to pull plows and carts. Some small farms and those in rural parts of the world still work this way. Farmers rely on draft animals that are known for their strength and ability to haul heavy loads. Draft animals include horses, oxen, donkeys, mules, and water buffalo. Using animal power to farm is greener than modern methods. But draft animals could never replace today's farming machines. They are not powerful enough to farm all the food needed to feed the world's population.

A farmer in India uses oxen to plow a field.

Spray irrigation

Drip irrigation

Drip irrigation systems can reduce a farm's water use by 60 percent.

## Water Savers

Farms need water for crops and animals. But when water from rivers and lakes is used for farms, there is less for people and wildlife. To save this important resource, some green farms capture rainwater in large tanks or ponds for later use.

Industrial farms waste water. They irrigate crops by spraying water onto plants. Heat from the sun causes a lot of that water to **evaporate** before it soaks into the ground. A greener method is drip irrigation. Long hoses or pipes with tiny holes slowly drip water right onto plants' roots, where it is needed.

## High-Tech Tools

Green farmers can use fewer natural resources by using technology to help check on crops. For example, remote-controlled drones with cameras can be flown over fields. They can look for signs of pests and weeds and see how well crops are growing. Sensors placed in the ground can detect when crops need irrigation. Companies are also working on autonomous farm machinery that operates itself. The machinery can be programmed to plow, plant, and harvest fields more efficiently than traditional machinery.

Some drones can be used to plant seeds.

## All Good!

Green farming can help keep Earth's soil healthy and its waterways free of chemical pollution and farm waste. It can improve the welfare of farm animals and wildlife. It can save energy, water, and other valuable resources. And best of all, it produces a healthier, wider range of food for people to enjoy!

Global sales of organic foods have increased in recent years.

Farmers' markets are great places to find organic foods.

Making good food choices is better for us and for the planet.

## A Sustainable Future

Green farming continues to grow. And more and more people are getting involved to help change agriculture for the better. Their goal is to sustainably feed our world in a way that is also good for the environment. Growing, buying, and eating food produced sustainably will help ensure a bright future for people, plants, and animals!

## Spot On!

# The University of Arizona Community Garden

**Many people live in apartments where they do not have space for a garden.** But, if they want, they can join a community garden instead. Community gardens allow neighbors to come together to grow their own food. And they can share resources like water, tools, and soil.

Many varieties of plants are grown in the University of Arizona Community Garden.

Captured rainwater is used to water plants.

Community gardens are also a great place to put green farming practices into action. At the University of Arizona Community Garden in Tucson, Arizona, people get hands-on experience doing just that. The garden uses a 28,000-gallon (106,000-liter) water tank to catch rainwater off a roof. A solar-powered pump delivers the water to the garden plants. There are many flowering plants to attract pollinators. A bat box provides roosts for native bat species, which also act as pollinators. Members also compost to create natural fertilizer for the garden beds.

# Make Compost

**Green farming is not just for farms.** Anyone with a garden, flower bed, or potted plants can use sustainable methods to help them grow. One easy way to do this is by making compost. It provides nutrients to plants to help them thrive. And it keeps waste out of landfills.

| DO Compost "Greens" | DO Compost "Browns" | Do Not Compost These |
|---|---|---|
| Food scraps (fruits, vegetables, and eggshells) | Old corn husks | General garbage |
| Lawn clippings | Dried leaves | Meat |
| Pulled weeds | Old newspapers/ paper towels/tissues/ coffee filters | Oils |
| Coffee grounds/ tea leaves | Dried straw/ hay | Dairy products (milk, cheese) |

## WHAT TO DO:

1. You will need a large plastic bin with a lid (to keep out animals). Ask an adult to cut a few small holes in the sides or top of the bin to let in air.
2. Find a clear area outdoors to place the bin. You can even set it on a balcony.
3. Whenever you have food scraps, such as orange peels and onion skins, place them in the bin. These are called "greens." Lawn clippings, pulled weeds, coffee grounds, and tea leaves are also greens.
4. Place a layer of "browns," like dried leaves, on top of your greens each time you add them to the bin. Then stir the compost with a tool, like a rake or shovel.
5. Once the bin is full, check on it every few days and give it a stir. Add a little bit of water to moisten the waste if it is dry.
6. Keep stirring the compost and adding water as indicated in Step 5. It will take about six months to a year for tiny microbes, worms, and insects to do their work and break down the material into compost. The compost is ready when it looks like crumbly black dirt. Add this natural fertilizer to any soil plants are growing in.

## True Statistics

**Number of acres of farmland in the world:** 12 billion

**Number of acres of organic farmland in the world:** 189 million (about 1.8 percent of total acres of farmland in the world)

**Number of cows, chickens, sheep, and pigs on Earth:** about 37 billion

**Total amount of money spent on organic food in the U.S. every year:** $60 billion

**Number of U.S. organic farms:** about 17,500

**Percent of people worldwide who make their livelihood from farming:** 27 percent

**Percent of the world's fresh water that goes to agriculture:** 70 percent

## Did you find the truth?

 **F** Organic food costs less than non-organic food.

 **T** Green farms avoid giving animals antibiotics.

# Resources

## Other books in this series:

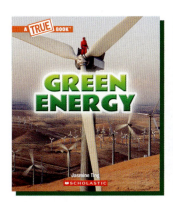
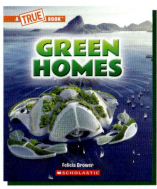
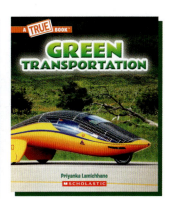

## You can also look at:

Brearley, Laurie. *Solar Power*. New York: Children's Press, 2019.

Castaldo, Nancy and Ginnie Hsu. *The Farm That Feeds Us: A year in the life of an organic farm*. Mission Viejo, CA: words & pictures, 2020.

Owings, Lisa. *From Garbage to Compost*. Minneapolis: Lerner Publications, 2016.

Rosinsky, Natalie M. *Dirt: The Scoop on Soil*. North Mankato, MN: Picture Window Books, 2003.

Squire, Ann O. *Grains and Cereals*. New York: Children's Press, 2017.

# Glossary

**arrays** (uh-RAYZ) large numbers of things

**climate change** (KLYE-mit CHAYNJ) global warming and other changes in the weather and weather patterns that are happening because of human activity

**compost** (KAHM-pohst) a mixture of organic material, such as rotted leaves, vegetables, or manure, that is added to soil to make it more productive

**evaporate** (i-VAP-uh-rate) to change into a vapor or gas

**fossil fuels** (FAH-suhl FYOO-uhlz) coal, oil, or natural gas formed from the remains of prehistoric plants and animals

**GMO** (JEE-em-oh) a plant or an animal that has been developed by changing its genetic makeup. *GMO* is short for "genetically modified organism."

**humane** (hyoo-MANE) not cruel to people or animals

**irrigate** (IR-uh-gate) to supply water to crops by artificial means, such as channels and pipes

**renewable** (ri-NOO-uh-buhl) can never be used up

**sustainable** (suh-STAY-nuh-buhl) done in a way that can be continued and that doesn't use up natural resources

**synthetic** (sin-THET-ik) manufactured or artificial rather than found in nature

**vaccinated** (VAK-suh-nay-tid) protected against a disease by receiving a dose of a vaccine

# Index

Page numbers in **bold** indicate illustrations.

animals for plowing/hauling, 35, **35**
animals, raising, 20–27, **20**, **22–23**, **25–27**
animal welfare, 21–23, **22–23**, 26, **26**
antibiotics, 26, **26**

chemical pesticides/herbicides, 13, **13**, 15, 17, 22, **24**, 25, 28
community gardens, 40–41, **40–41**
compost, farming with, 12, **12**, 41
compost, making, 42–43, **42–43**
costs of farming, 28–29, **28–29**
cover crops, 15, **15**, 29
cows and methane, 27, **27**
crops, growing, 10–17, **10**, **12–17**, 29, 36, **36**

diseases in livestock, 26, **26**
drones, 37, **37**

electric tractors, 34, **34**
equipment, eco-friendly, 30–34, **30**, **32–34**, 36–37, **36–37**

farming history, **24–25**
farming overview, 6–11, **6–10**
fertilizers, 12, **12**, 14

green farming benefits, 19, **19**, 38–39, **38–39**
green farming costs, 28–29, **28–29**
green farming overview, 8–9, **8–9**, 11
greenhouse gases, 27, **27**

honeybees, 25, **25**
hydroponic farming, 18, **18**

livestock, 20–27, **20**, **22–23**, **25–27**

manure, 12, **12**, 24, 27

natural fertilizers, 12, **12**, 24, 28, 41

organic certification/farming, 17, **17**, 22, **22**, **24**, **25**, 28–29, **38**
organic livestock, 22, **22**

pest control, 13, **13**

renewable energy, 30–33, **30**, **32–33**
rooftop gardens, 19, **19**
rotation of crops, 14, **14**, 29

single-crop farming, 11, 14, 29
solar panels/arrays, **9**, 32, **32**
synthetic fertilizers, 12, **12**, 17, 28

technological tools, 37, **37**
tractors, electric, 34, **34**

University of Arizona Community Garden, 40–41, **40–41**
urban farming, 18–19, **18–19**

vaccinations, 26, **26**

waste of livestock (manure), 12, **12**, 24, 27
water conservation, 18, **18**, 19, **19**, 36, **36**, 41, **41**
weed control, 15, **15**
wind power, 30–31, **30**, 33, **33**

## About the Authors

Daniel Johnson and Samantha Johnson are a brother-sister writing team, and together they've written more than a dozen nonfiction books. They have farmed in Wisconsin using green methods for more than 20 years and especially love growing colorful varieties of tomatoes. Daniel has a particular interest in solar energy, and Samantha loves heritage livestock breeds. Samantha was the grand prize winner of the 2009 Native Insight writing competition.

Photos ©: cover: Patrick Hertzog/AFP/Getty Images; back cover: GomezDavid/Getty Images; 3: pixdeluxe/Getty Images; 4: Independent Picture Service/Alamy Images; 5 top: John Deere; 6–7: ArtistGNDphotography/Getty Images; 8–9: Manfred Gottschalk/Alamy Images; 12 left: Westend61/Getty Images; 12 right: Me 3645 Studio/Getty Images; 13 right: GomezDavid/Getty Images; 14 left: Gary J Weathers/Getty Images; 15: mvburling/Getty Images; 17: Brian Green/Alamy Images; 19 bottom: fotografixx/Getty Images; 20–21: pixdeluxe/Getty Images; 22: Toltek/Getty Images; 23: pidjoe/Getty Images; 24 left: Gianni Dagli Orti/Shutterstock; 24 center: CTK/AP Images; 25 bottom left: Independent Picture Service/Alamy Images; 25 bottom right: Hill Street Studios/Getty Images; 26: Jevtic/Getty Images; 27: PeopleImages/Getty Images; 28–29: coldsnowstorm/Getty Images; 30–31: Daniel Balakov/Getty Images; 32: panaramka/Getty Images; 33: raclro/Getty Images; 34: John Deere; 36 left: demachi/Getty Images; 36 right: mgstudyo/Getty Images; 40–41 background: billnoll/Getty Images; 40: Moses Thompson; 41: Ashley Limbaugh.

All other photos © Shutterstock.